Searchlight
BOOKS™

Fear Fest

Chilling

Ancient
Curses

Tracy Nelson Maurer

Lerner Publications ◆ Minneapolis

For Mike,
my charmer

Lerner Publications Company
A division of Lerner Publishing Group, Inc.
241 First Avenue North
Minneapolis, MN 55401 USA

For reading levels and more information, look up this title
at www.lernerbooks.com.

Library of Congress Cataloging-in-Publication Data

Names: Maurer, Tracy, 1965– author.
Title: Chilling ancient curses / Tracy Nelson Maurer.
Description: Minneapolis : Lerner Publications, 2017. | Series: Searchlight Books™
    — Fear Fest | Includes bibliographical references and index.
Identifiers: LCCN 2016051844 (print) | LCCN 2017006207 (ebook) | ISBN
    9781512434033 (lb : alk. paper) | ISBN 9781512456035 (pb : alk. paper) | ISBN
    9781512450743 (eb pdf)
Subjects: LCSH: Incantations—Juvenile literature. | Blessing and cursing—Juvenile
    literature.
Classification: LCC BF1558 .M35 2017 (print) | LCC BF1558 (ebook) | DDC 133.4/4—dc23
LC record available at https://lccn.loc.gov/2016051844

Manufactured in the United States of America
2-45898-23909-4/27/2018

Contents

Chapter 1

WHAT IS A CURSE?

Imagine that you found a locked treasure chest in a dark corner of your attic. Under a thick layer of dust and cobwebs, a chilling curse was carved into the old, wooden top. It said, "Those who dare to open the chest will be cursed with bad luck for all of their days."

Would you open the chest?

Physical objects, such as this chest, are sometimes said to be cursed. What else can be cursed?

Powerful Words

Many stories over the centuries have told of cursed people, places, or things. For those who believe in curses, the words carry power to promise harm, sickness, bad luck, or even death. The threats and warnings curses contained scared people out of making bad choices.

Ancient Egyptians used hieroglyphs as their writing system. There were often curses carved into the limestone of buildings and landmarks that warned great harm would come to thieves.

In Norway and Iceland, ancient Norsemen used objects called nithing poles to curse their enemies. They pointed the pole at the enemy to curse them. This was a terrible insult used only in the most serious situations.

A nithing pole is a long pole covered in ancient letters called runes. A horse skull sat on top of the pole. A

nithing pole was said to drive King Eric Bloodaxe and his queen from Norway to the British Isles in the tenth century.

Some people still believe in the power of the nithing pole. Protesters in Iceland put fish skulls on nithing poles in early 2016 and pointed them at the prime minister's home to curse him for lying about his finances. He soon left office. Was that the nithing pole at work?

A nithing pole was planted in the ground and pointed at enemies to curse them. This was considered a serious insult.

fact or fiction?

Curses are the same as spells, hexes, and jinxes.

That's a fact—sort of.

Curses are a type of magical spell believed to bring illness (or worse!) to someone. People say curses can last for centuries and affect entire countries.

Hexes are supposed to cause general bad luck. They are cast like spells, usually by people thought to have magical power.

Jinxes are the least harmful and often the shortest kind of curse. Any person or event can set off a jinx.

Some athletes think they will jinx a winning streak if they change their socks.

Curses at Work

Cheating, trespassing, boasting, or just acting unkind could bring on a curse, according to many old tales. Sometimes the curse fits the crime. Perhaps someone who lied would lose the ability to speak. Or a murderer would die an early death.

A curse for trespassing might cause a person to be locked up or frozen and unable to move freely.

A curse could also warn against stealing or breaking laws. Between 668 and 627 BCE, the king of Assyria used a curse to protect his huge library of clay tablets from thieves. The curse promised the destructive "wrath and anger" of the gods to anyone who stole his tablets. That's some library fine!

THE CURSES ON THE TABLETS IN THE ANCIENT ASSYRIAN CITY OF NINEVEH ARE THE EARLIEST KNOWN BOOK CURSE.

Chapter 2

HOW OLD ARE CURSES?

Curses seem to be tangled with unexplained events throughout human history. A few curses stretch across time. They pass from one generation to the next. So even though a great-great-grandson had nothing to do with hunting on a king's land three hundred years ago, some people believe he would still inherit the old curse. Nobody said curses were fair!

Ravens have been kept at the Tower of London for hundreds of years because of an old curse. Can curses be passed on?

The Mummy's Curse

One of the most famous—and deadly—ancient curses is said to protect the treasures and the mummy of the Egyptian pharaoh Tutankhamun. Howard Carter found his tomb in November 1922.

The tomb reportedly came with a warning to let the king rest in peace, saying anyone who didn't would meet certain death. After Carter unsealed the pharaoh's tomb, stories about the curse spread.

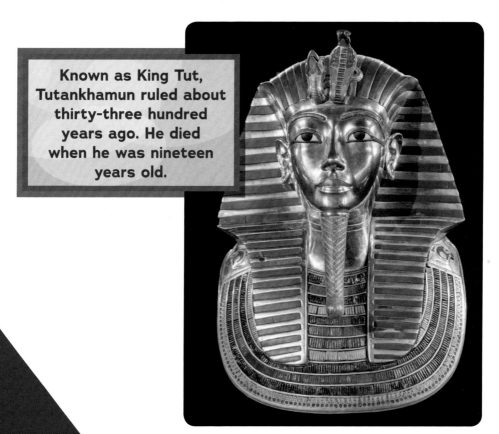

Known as King Tut, Tutankhamun ruled about thirty-three hundred years ago. He died when he was nineteen years old.

People claimed that a cobra ate Carter's pet canary the night he opened the tomb. Cobras were thought to protect the pharaohs.

Fevers, poison, heatstroke, suicide, and murder—the mummy's curse had killed twenty-one people connected to King Tut by 1935, according to the press of the day. Some researchers believe that number is closer to eight. No one knows if they would have died even if the mummy had not been disturbed. Do you think it was the curse at work?

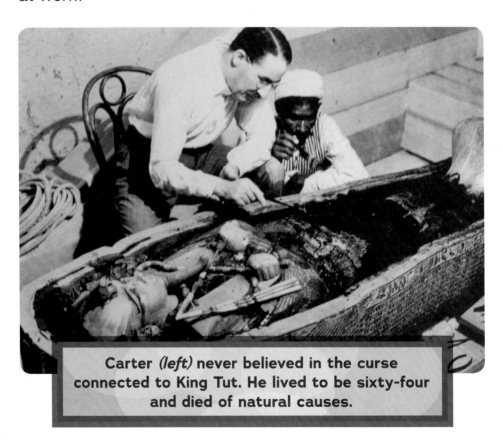

Carter *(left)* never believed in the curse connected to King Tut. He lived to be sixty-four and died of natural causes.

Fact or Fiction?

The oldest known curses come from ancient Egypt.

Fact!

No one knows for sure when people began setting curses. Some of the best examples come from Egypt more than three thousand years ago.

Nobody could read the Egyptian hieroglyphs for centuries. In 1819, a British mathematician named Thomas Young began to decode the symbols. French scholar Jean-François Champollion eventually developed the system used to decipher the ancient Egyptian writing using the famous Rosetta Stone.

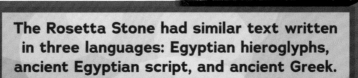

The Rosetta Stone had similar text written in three languages: Egyptian hieroglyphs, ancient Egyptian script, and ancient Greek.

Chapter 3

WHO MAKES OR BREAKS CURSES?

In ancient times, anyone could curse another person. People believed to be witches or wizards, royalty, priests, and gods might conjure more powerful curses.

The good news? Curses could be broken. Some said that the most dependable way to break a curse was to undo the bad deed. So if you'd stolen something, giving back the stolen item could lift the curse.

There are many stories of pirates being cursed after stealing buried treasure. How might they break the curse?

Thieves have often returned cursed items. In 2015, a museum in Israel found two two-thousand-year-old Roman sling stones in the courtyard with a note from the robber. It said the weapons brought trouble.

Hiring help to break a curse was another option. Worried folks have paid Romany mystics to supposedly break curses, cast spells, or tell the future. It is hard to say if or why the Romany people are thought to be especially good at breaking curses.

Herbs and plants were often used to break curses.

Curses around the World

Nearly every culture, or group of people, has believed in the power of curses at one time. The Inuit people of North America and Greenland turned to secret *tupilaq* dolls to carry curses to their enemies. But they had to be very careful! The curse could come back to the person who made it.

Slaves brought to America from Africa and the Caribbean practiced voodoo, which used a doll called a poppet to cast spells. Marie Laveau from New Orleans, Louisiana, was famous for her curses. If someone found one of her poppets on the doorstep or in a purse, the terrified victim would soon ask her to lift the curse.

Tupilaq dolls were often made of animal parts like bone and hair.

fact or fiction?

You can be cursed just by someone looking at you.

That's a fact, if you believe it.

Around the world, people have thought that the evil eye curse can cause bad luck, injury, illness, and other misfortune. The curse is cast by glaring at the victim, especially when the person is not aware of it.

People in such places as Greece, Egypt, Turkey, Iran, Iraq, Italy, and Afghanistan wear charms and discs painted to look like an eye to ward off the curse. These protective decorations are called *nazars*.

Nazars are still sold in tourist shops in areas of the Mediterranean region and the Middle East.

A Country's Curse

Sometimes a curse affects an entire country! In about 1000 CE, Hungary was supposedly cursed by a shaman who refused the king's religious orders. The curse was called the Curse of Turan and was said to have lasted for a thousand years. It was blamed for all kinds of bad luck and tragedy there. Hungary lost to invading forces many times, suffering devastating losses in wars with the Mongols, Turks, Austrians, Russians, and Romanians over the centuries. The one thousand years of the curse are over, and there have been no more invasions. Coincidence?

Stephen I of Hungary was the king responsible for giving the religious orders that led to the country being cursed.

In the United States, Tecumseh's Curse began when the American Indian warrior Tecumseh lost the Battle of Tippecanoe against William Henry Harrison's troops. Soldiers claimed Tecumseh cursed Harrison and the US presidents who followed.

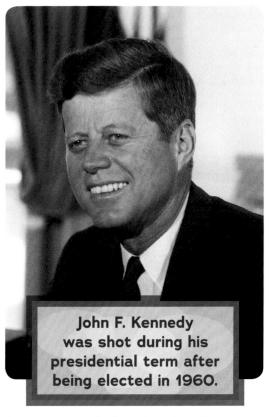

John F. Kennedy was shot during his presidential term after being elected in 1960.

Elected in 1840, Harrison died one month after his inauguration. If you believe it, the curse has caused the death of every US president elected or reelected every twenty years from 1840 to 1960. Then, Ronald Reagan, who was elected in 1980, was shot but survived. Perhaps that helped to lift the curse. George W. Bush, who was elected in 2000, lived through two full terms.

Sports Curses

Some ancient curses were specific to sports. Ancient Greeks and Romans often tried to curse their opponents. They wanted to win no matter what. Chariot races, wrestling matches, and gladiator events meant privilege and fame for the winners. The losers might be forced into slavery or even killed.

With so much on the line, athletes sometimes buried lead curse tablets near where the games or races were held. Some curses were intended to cause the other competitor to simply fall down and make a fool of himself. Others were more graphic, perhaps asking the curse to chop the charioteer and his horse into bits. Talk about poor sportsmanship!

With the high stakes of gladiator events, the athletes were willing to curse their opponent to avoid losing.

Wrigley Field and the Great Goat Curse

Not all sports curses are ancient. In 1945, William Sianis brought his pet goat to Wrigley Field to see the Chicago Cubs baseball team play in a World Series game. When officials made Sianis leave with his goat, he reportedly cursed the team and vowed the Cubs would never win a

World Series. They didn't—until 2016! The last time the Cubs had won a championship was 1908. No other major-league team ever went that long without a title. What broke the curse? No one knows for sure.

The Cubs defied the curse by winning four of the seven games in the 2016 World Series.

Chapter 4

IS THERE PROOF?

People often point to curses when they need to explain why bad things have happened. Perhaps that's how the Curse of the Hope Diamond began. The world's largest blue diamond was said to have been pried from the eye of a religious statue in India. The theft angered the gods and brought down the curse on all who own the treasure to suffer chaos, agony, or unexpected death . . . or so the legend goes.

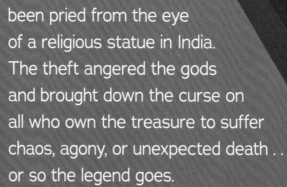

Chaos and ruin struck all the Hope Diamond's owners. Marie Antoinette and her husband, King Louis XVI of France, were both executed. But is that proof?

Perhaps jeweler Pierre Cartier encouraged the tale after he bought the diamond in 1910. In 1911, he sold the gem to Evalyn Walsh McLean, a wealthy American heiress, tempting her with stories of the stone's cursed past.

Later, McLean's son died in a car accident at the age of nine. Her daughter overdosed on sleeping pills. Her husband left her and died in an asylum. The family went bankrupt. Was that proof? Often what seems like evidence could be a coincidence. Even McLean still didn't believe the diamond was truly cursed, only that her life took many tragic turns.

Evalyn Walsh McLean didn't believe in the curse and wore the Hope Diamond for years.

SCARAB AMULETS WERE USED IN MANY ANCIENT EGYPTIAN RITUALS TO OFFER PROTECTION.

Just in Case

Are curses real? People have worn amulets and talismans for thousands of years just in case. The pharaohs and other Egyptians wore jewelry to guard against evil and bring good luck. A common talisman was the scarab beetle. Egyptians were often buried with a beetle charm placed on their heart to protect them in the afterlife.

Ancient Romans gave their children special amulets to keep them safe. For centuries, people in China have worn jewelry carved with symbols to protect them or bring good luck. Maybe you've knocked on wood to ward off bad luck . . . just in case?

Fact or Fiction?

Charm bracelets bring good luck.

Fact or not, it's worth a try!

Charm bracelets have been popular at different times over the centuries. The idea is that you can wear a collection of small charms to ward off bad luck. Some think the clinking noises these metal bracelets make scare off evil. Do charm bracelets really work? Who knows?

Crossing your fingers, rabbit's feet, good luck charms, and more have all been used to keep bad luck away.

Modern Curses

People are tempted to believe in the power of curses. Many people still wear talismans, such as birthstones that are thought to bring good luck with their birth month.

Other good luck charms include smooth stones, special coins, or four-leaf clovers. Do you have a lucky charm?

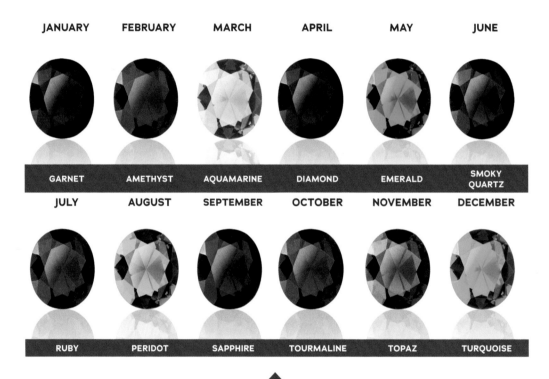

JANUARY	FEBRUARY	MARCH	APRIL	MAY	JUNE
GARNET	AMETHYST	AQUAMARINE	DIAMOND	EMERALD	SMOKY QUARTZ

JULY	AUGUST	SEPTEMBER	OCTOBER	NOVEMBER	DECEMBER
RUBY	PERIDOT	SAPPHIRE	TOURMALINE	TOPAZ	TURQUOISE

BIRTHSTONES ARE COMMON IN NECKLACES AND EARRINGS. A DIFFERENT BIRTHSTONE IS CONNECTED TO EACH MONTH OF THE YEAR.

Some people think iron horseshoes are especially powerful for warding off misfortune. Perhaps they believe the strong metal symbolizes protection. The horseshoe's shape looks like a new crescent moon, which is thought to be a sign of good things to come. For centuries, people have nailed horseshoes above their doors, but not everyone agrees on which way to display them. Does the horseshoe face up like a *U* to hold good luck for the home? Or does the open end face down to pour good fortune on those who pass under it? It's all what you believe!

A four-leaf clover is rare, and finding one is said to bring you good luck.

The Koh-i-Noor diamond that sits in the Crown Jewels of the United Kingdom is said to have its own curse.

Do Ancient Curses Exist?

Researchers think that perhaps it doesn't matter if curses are real if people believe in them.

Maybe the truth is that some people are just unlucky. Maybe some things just happen by coincidence. Or maybe science can explain some curses. For example, perhaps ancient mold found in the Egyptian tombs was the reason people who opened them died. Still, skeptics question why a curse affects some people but not everyone, as in the case of King Tut's tomb.

Even so, many people over time have chosen not to risk a curse. Would you?

Believe It or Not!

- According to some, you can accidentally curse yourself!

- A full moon is believed to make a curse more powerful. People still report strange things happening when there is a full moon.

- Gold and silver curse tablets were discovered in Serbia in 2016 buried in ancient Roman graves.

- Harry Winston bought the Hope Diamond and donated it to the Smithsonian Institution in 1958. It is the museum's most popular display. Some people think that if America owns the Hope Diamond, the country is cursed. Do you believe that?

Glossary

amulet: a small piece of jewelry thought to protect the wearer

coincidence: when events or circumstances happen that appear related but aren't

conjure: to make happen

decipher: to figure out

evidence: facts that prove something is true or not

gladiator: an armed competitor in violent Roman games

hieroglyph: a character, or letter, in an ancient Egyptian writing system

nazar: a protection against the evil eye curse

nithing pole: a Germanic, Norse, or Viking cursing pole, also called a *niding* pole, or *nidstang*

opponent: a rival or competitor

poppet: a doll used for curses or other spells

Romany: a group of people originally from northern India who live mainly in Asia, Europe, and North America

rune: part of a system of ancient letters, especially in ancient Nordic countries

talisman: an item or symbol thought to protect the owner

trespass: to go where one is not allowed

Learn More about Ancient Curses

Books

Doeden, Matt. *Tools and Treasures of Ancient Egypt.* Minneapolis: Lerner Publications, 2014. Read all about hieroglyphs, mummies, and the pyramids. Find out what tools the ancient Egyptians used to create the treasures that still exist.

Kelly, David A. *Babe Ruth and the Baseball Curse: How the Red Sox Curse Became a Legend.* New York: Random House, 2009. Baseball fans will love to read about Babe Ruth's curse and how it haunted the Red Sox for more than eighty years.

Westphal, Jeremy. *The Mummy's Curse.* Minneapolis: Bellwether, 2012. Learn more about the curses that keep watch over the tombs of Egypt's pharaohs.

Websites

Ancient History: Mesopotamia
http://mesopotamia.mrdonn.org/library.html
This link brings you to the Ancient Mesopotamia page, but the site is full of ancient history information!

History for Kids: Ancient Egyptian Artifacts
http://www.historyforkids.net/egyptian-artifacts.html
Discover ancient Egyptian information as well as articles about other countries and regions.

PBS: The Notorious Hope Diamond
http://www.pbs.org/treasuresoftheworld/a_nav/hope_nav/main_hopfrm.html
Learn fun facts about the Hope Diamond from the researchers at the Public Broadcasting Service (PBS).

Index

Photo Acknowledgments

The images in this book are used with the permission of: © iStockphoto.com/sb-borg, p. 4; © Jakub Kync/Shutterstock.com, p. 5; Fernando Alvarez Charro/Alamy Stock Photo, p. 6; © shironosov/iStock/Thinkstock, p. 7; © Jupiterimages/PHOTOS.com/Thinkstock, p. 8; Zev Radovan/BibleLandPictures/Alamy Stock Photo, p. 9; © Anna Kucherova/Shutterstock.com, p. 10; Julia Hiebaum/Alamy Stock Photo, p. 11; Frank Miesnikowicz/Alamy Stock Photo, p. 12; © Brand X Pictures/Stockbyte/Thinkstock, p. 13; © grafvision/iStock/Thinkstock, p. 14; © successo images/Shutterstock.com, p. 15; Desmond Morris Collection/World History Archive/Alamy Stock Photo, p. 16; © irinaorel/iStock/Thinkstock, p. 17; © Ingram Publishing/Thinkstock, p. 18; ©Cecil Stoughton, White House/Wikimedia Commons (public domain), p. 19; © GTS Productions/Shutterstock.com, p. 20; ERIK S. LESSER/EPA/Newscom, p. 21; Fine Art Images/Heritage Image Partnership Ltd/Alamy Stock Photo, p. 22; Everett Collection Historical/Alamy Stock Photo, p. 23; © Daniil Kirillov/Hemera/Thinkstock, p. 24; Frankie Angel/Alamy Stock Photo, p. 25; JewelryStock/Alamy Stock Photo, p. 26; © Kyoichi Otsu/iStock/Thinkstock, p. 27; © GraphicaArtis/Archive Photos/Getty Images, p. 28.

Front cover: © iStockphoto.com/blackred (grunge frame texture); Barry Iverson/Alamy Stock Photo (mummy).

Main body text set in Adrianna Regular 14/20.
Typeface provided by Chank.